Johannes Brahms
(1833-1897)

Variationen

für Klavier · for piano · pour piano

Urtext

Herausgegeben von · Edited by · Edité par
Enikő Gyenge
K 115
Könemann Music Budapest

INDEX

Frau Clara Schumann zugeeignet

Variationen in fis

über ein Thema von Robert Schumann

Thema

Ziemlich langsam

Op. 9
Düsseldorf, 1854

Var. I

Var. III

Tempo di tema

Var. IV

Poco più moto

8

Var. VII

Andante

Var. VIII

Andante (non troppo lento)

Var. XI

Var. XII

Allegretto, poco scherzando

K 115

Var. XIII

Non troppo presto

Var. XV

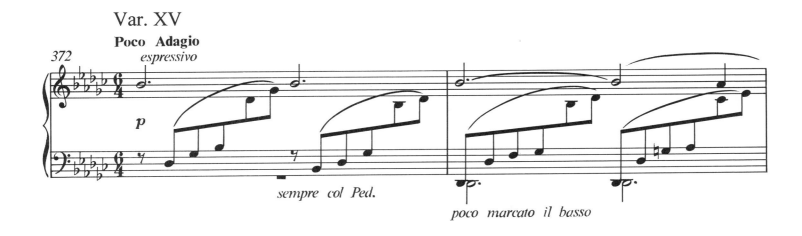

Variationen in D

über ein eigenes Thema

Op. 21, No. 1
Düsseldorf, 1856

Thema
Poco larghetto

K 115

Var. II
Più moto

Var. V

Tempo di tema

molto dolce

teneramente

p

Canone in moto contrario

molto espressivo

legato

sempre col Ped.

Var. VI

Più moto

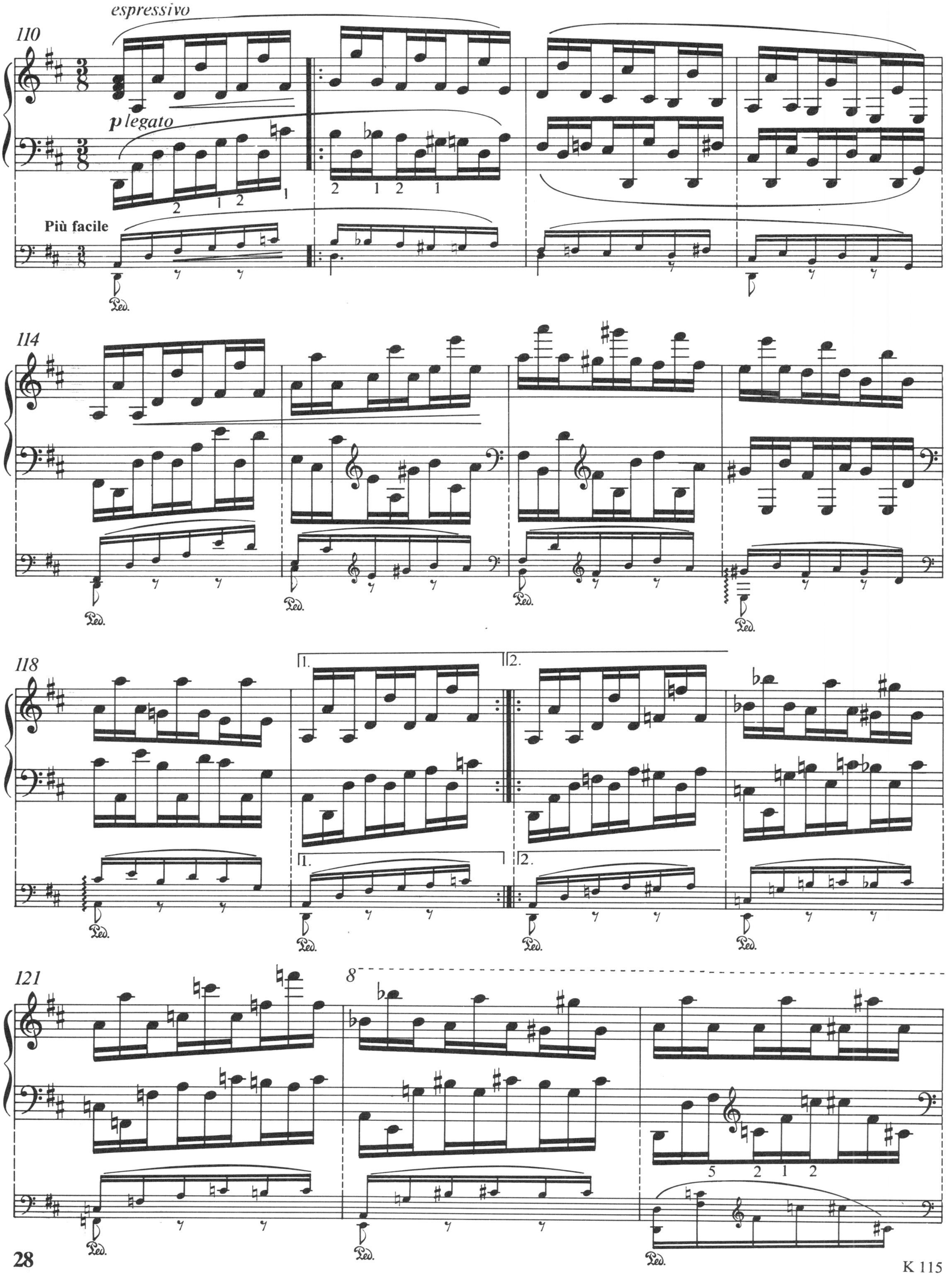

Var. VII

Andante con moto

Var. VIII

Allegro non troppo

30

Variationen in D

über ein ungarisches Lied

Op. 21, No. 2

sempre molto marcato

42

44

Variationen und Fuge in B

über ein Thema von Händel

Op. 24
Hamburg, 1861

46

K 115

Var. II

Var. III

Var. IV

Var. V

Var. VI *legato*

Var. VII *con vivacità*

Var. VIII

Var. IX

poco sostenuto

Var. X

Var. XI

Var. XII

Var. XIII

Largamente, ma non più

Var. XIV

Var. XV

Var. XVI

Var. XVII

Var. XIX

59

Var. XX

Var. XXI

Var. XXII

Var. XXIII

Var. XXV

Fuga

col Ped.

f

Variationen in a

über ein Thema von Paganini

"Studien für Pianoforte", Op. 35/I
Wien, 1862-63

Thema

Presto

Var. III

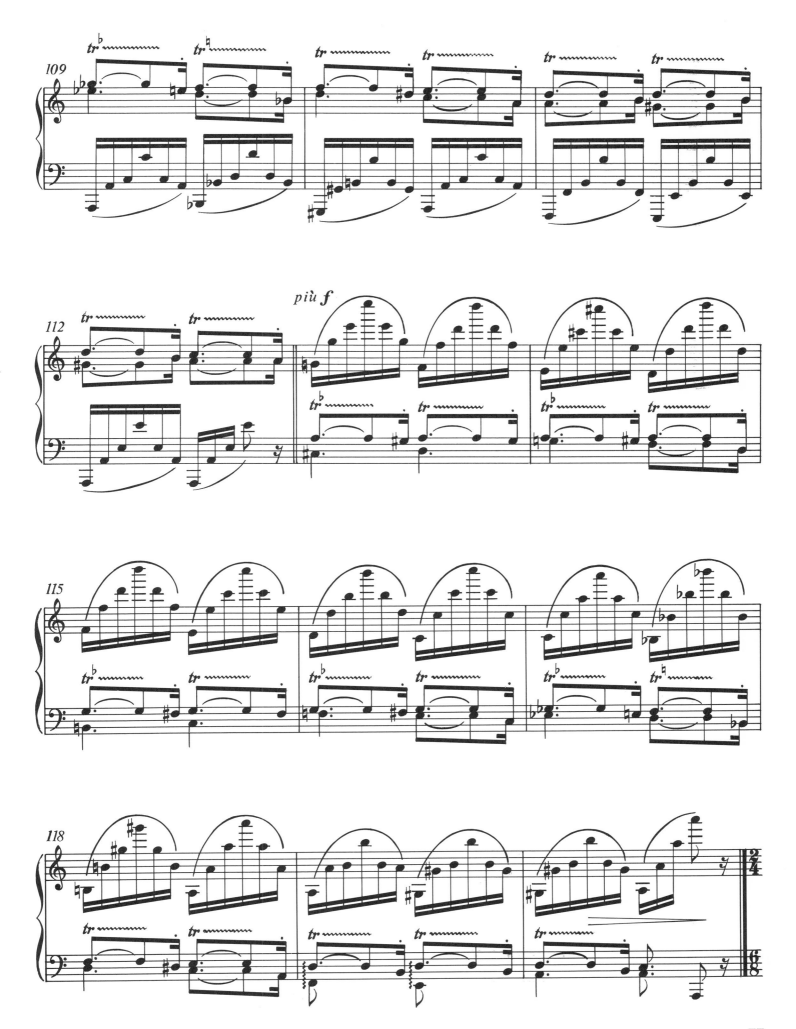

Var. VII

Var. VIII

Var. IX

Var. XI
Andante
218
pp
tutti molto legato e dolce
p espress.
222
pp una corda
226
pp tre corde
p espress.
230
1.
2.
ritard.
Var. XII
234
p
molto dolce, 2ª volta pp

Var. XIII

Presto, ma non troppo

Variationen in a

über ein Thema von Paganini

"Studien für Pianoforte", Op. 35/II

Thema

Non troppo presto

Var. II
Poco animato

Var. IV

Var. IX

Var. X

Feroce, energico

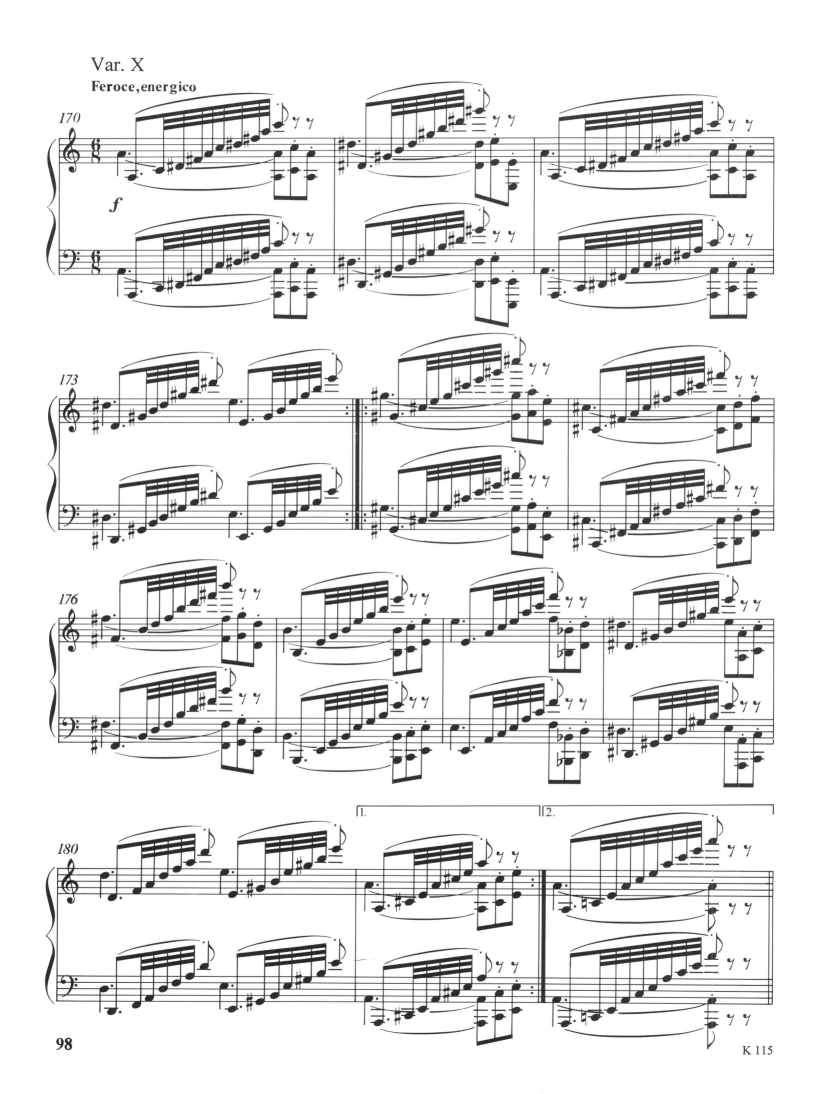

K 115

Var. XIII

Un poco più Andante

Var. XIV

Presto, ma non troppo

Appendix

Clara Schumann zugeeignet
Zum 13. September 1860 als freundlichen Gruß

Thema mit Variationen

Op. 18/II
Hamburg–Bonn, 1860

Notes

The variation, which in the works of the Romantic composer-performenrs lingered on chiefly as the principle underlying the paraphrases of popular melodies, returned in the piano variations of Brahms to the form and function it had in Bach and Beethoven. Beginning with the slow movement of the Op. 1 Piano Sonata, numerous piano, chamber and orchestral works were written in terms of variation form. The composer, who spoke extremely rarely about his compositional methods, provides us with unusual and interesting information concerning his own variation technique in a letter written to his friend Adolf Schubring (17th February 1869): 'Bei einem Thema zu Variationen bedeutet mir *eigentlich,* fast, beinahe nur der Bass etwas. Aber dieser ist mir heilig, er ist der feste Grund, auf dem ich dann meine Geschichten baue. Was ich mit der Melodie mache, ist nur Spielerei oder geistreiche – Spielerei. ... Über den gegebenen Bass erfinde ich wirklich neu, ich erfinde ihm neue Melodien, ich schaffe.'

The present volume contains all the variations Brahms composed for the piano. The composer's own arrangement of the slow movement of the Op. 18 String Sextet, reflecting as it does the authentic musical and instrumental conception of Brahms, is given as an appendix at the end. The Op. 23 set (Variations on a Theme of Schumann for 4 hands) has not been included, the version for 2 hands being an arrangement by Theodor Kirchner.

This edition is based on the autographs of the variations, and/or copies of early editions revised by the composer.

Editorial additions have been reduced to a minimum, and given in small print in square brackets. Exceptions are a few warning accidentals and clef changes added to assist in a smoother reading of the score. Also replaced without comment are the markings which were absent in the manuscript, but which Brahms added either for the first edition, or later wrote into his printed copy (Handexemplar).

Editorial additions based upon analogous passages of music have not been included. No suggestions concerning performance, the execution of ornaments or fingering have been given. The titles and dedications of works are given as they appear in the sources.

Where the sources contradict each other in important areas, then the version found in the composer's Handexemplar has been taken as a guide. The alternatives and equally valid versions that arose are detailed below.

1. Variations on a Theme of R. Schumann, Op. 9

Theme: the first piece from the set of five Albumblätter in Schumann's Bunte Blätter Op. 99.
Sources:
  A: Autograph (Österreichische Nationalbibliothek, Wien, PhA 308)
  B: Composer's copy (Handexemplar) of the 1854 first edition (Breitkopf & Härtel, Leipzig, plate number 9001), a copy revised by the composer (Gesellschaft der Musikfreunde, Wien, Nachlass Brahms).
  C: Handexemplar of the 1875 omnibus volume (Breitkopf & Härtel, Leipzig, plate number 13598), a copy revised by the composer (Gesellschaft der Musikfreunde, Wien, Nachlass Luithlen-Kalbeck, VII 41553).

Var. VII, bar 183, lower voice, 3rd beat: ⌢ is an editorial addition.
  bar 188: time signature given as found in sources.
Var. VIII, bar 202, upper voice, 4th quaver: arpeggio only in **A**.
Var. X: tempo marking in **A**: *Molto Andante*.
  bars 238, 262, 266, upper voice, 2nd beat: this original notation suggests a performance with even and uneven rhythms.
  bar 247: arpeggio only in **B**.
Var. XIV: tempo marking in **A**: *Poco Andante*.
Var. XV, bar 373: *un poco marcato il basso* missing in **B**.
  bar 383, middle voice, 6th and 12th quavers: without accidental in all sources.
  bar 388: *in tempo* only in **A**.
  bar 397: *dim.* only in **A**.
Var. XVI: *Adagio* only in **A**.

2. Variations on an Original Theme Op. 21, No. 1

Source consulted for this edition: Handexemplar of 1862 first edition (N.Simrock, Bonn, plate number 6203), a copy revised by the composer (Gesellschaft der Musikfreunde, Wien, Nachlass Brahms).

Theme, bar 17, upper voice 1st quaver *b¹* without correction. In later editions – also in the present one – emended to *a¹*.

Var. XI, bar 237, upper voice: a quaver rest missing.

3. Variations on a Hungarian Song Op. 21, No. 2

Theme: 'Ez a kis lány hamis kis lány' (This girl is a saucy creature), found in Bartalus-Füredi: 101 nép és magyar dal, Pest 1861, 5. (101 Folk- and Hungarian Songs, [Buda-]Pest, 1861, 5.)

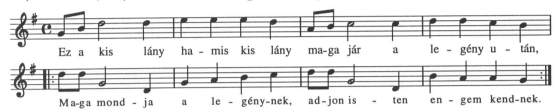

Sources:
- **A**: Autograph, Musiksammlung der Wiener Stadt- und Landesbibliothek, MH 4029/c.
- **B**: Handexemplar of the 1862 first edition (N.Simrock, Bonn plate number 6204). The score contains no subsequent corrections by the composer, but differs slightly from **A**. (Gesellschaft der Musikfreunde, Wien, Nachlass Brahms).

Var. VIII: tempo marking only in **A**.

Var X: all bars in **A** with ⎯⎯ . In **B** and in the present edition omitted.

Bar 177: tempo marking *Poco meno Presto* only in **A**.

Bar 189: tempo marking *Tempo I^{mo}* only in **A**.

4. Variations and Fugue on a Theme of Händel Op. 24

Theme: Aria, originally with 5 variations (HHA IV/5, 5), from book 2 of the Suites de pièces pour le Clavecin.

Sources:
- **A**: Copy of the autograph consulted, number PhA 278 in the Österreichische Nationalbibliothek, Wien.
- **B**: Handexemplar of the 1862 first edition (Breitkopf & Härtel, Leipzig, plate number 10448), a copy without corrections by the composer (Gesellschaft der Musikfreunde, Wien, Nachlass Brahms).
- **C**: Handexemplar of the 1875 omnibus edition (Breitkopf & Härtel, Leipzig, plate number 13598), a copy corrected by the composer (Gesellschaft der Musikfreunde, Wien).

The dedication on the Manuscript (*Variationen für eine liebe Freundin*) is to Clara Schumann.

Var. VII, bar 61, at the beginning *mf* a correction of *p* in **A**. In **B** and **C** no dynamic mark.

Var. XIII, bar 121, upper voice, last beat, note *f* in **B** a quaver.

Var. XIX, bar 174: *p* only in **A**.

Var. XXIV, bars 232-233, upper voice in **A**:

Fugue, bar 255, lower stave 1st beat in **A**:

bar 272 1st and 3rd beats: chords in **A** and **B** with arpeggio. Here given as found in **C**.

bars 336-338: the slurs are autograph additions in **C**.

5. **Studien für Klavier**
   Variations on a Theme of Paganini Op. 35
   Books I and II

Theme: Paganini's Caprice in A minor for violin, Op. 1, No. 24.

Sources:
    A: Autograph of Book I, photocopy consulted, numbered PhA 283 in the Österreichische Nationalbibliothek, Wien.
    B: Manuscript copy signed by Brahms of Books I and II (Gesellschaft der Musikfreunde, Wien).
    C: The composer's Handexemplar, a copy of the first edition (J.Rieter-Biedermann, Leipzig & Winterthur, 1866, plate number 436 a.b.) revised by Brahms. (Gesellschaft der Musikfreunde, Wien, Nachlass Brahms.)

Book I

Tempo markings of the theme and the 1st variation are given here as pencilled into **C** by Brahms.

Var. II, last chord in all sources has fermata. In **C** deleted in pencil.

Book II

Var. I: tempo marking in **B**: *Allegro.*
Var. VII, bar 138: *leggiero* taken from **C**.
Var. XIII: fingering given as added to **C**.

Appendix

6. Theme and Variations Op. 18, 2nd movement

The piano arrangement of the second movement of the Op. 18 String Sextet, which according to the dedication and date was made for Clara Schumann as a birthday present in 1860.

Source: The autograph consulted in the *Collected Facsimiles: Johannes Brahms: opus 24 / opus 23 / opus 18 / opus 90.* The Robert Owen Lehmann Foundation, New York 1967.

bar 16, upper voice, 2nd beat: originally a quaver.

KÖNEMANN MUSIC BUDAPEST
Juli 1998

PÄDAGOGISCHE AUSGABEN
für Klavier
PEDAGOGICAL EDITIONS
for piano

Pekka Vapaavuori–Hannele Hynninen:

Der Barockpianist – *The Baroque Pianist*

PIANO STEP BY STEP

Alte Tänze – *Early Dances*
Beethoven: 47 Piano Pieces
Einführung in das polyphone Spiel – *Introduction to Polyphonic Playing*
Erste Konzertstücke I–II–III–IV – *First Concert Pieces I–II–III–IV*
Etüden
Haydn: 23 Piano Pieces
Mozart: 44 Piano Pieces
Sonatinen I–II–III
Vierhändige Klaviermusik – *Works for Piano Duet I–II*

IN VORBEREITUNG – *IN PREPARATION*
Vierhändige Klaviermusik – *Works for Piano Duet III*

FAVOURITE PIANO STUDIES

Karl Czerny:

100 Übungsstücke – *100 Exercises,* Op. 139
Die Schule der Geläufigkeit – *The School of Velocity,* Op. 299
Kunst der Fingerfertigkeit – *The Art of Finger Dexterity* I–II, Op. 740

FAVOURITES for piano

American Classical Songs I–II
Favourite Piano Classics I–II
Favourite Opera Classics I–II (Mozart)
Favourite Opera Classics III–IV (Verdi)
Scott Joplin: Ragtimes
Spirituals
Johann Strauss: Walzer

IN VORBEREITUNG – *IN PREPARATION*
American Classical Songs III
Favourite Piano Classics III–IV
100 deutsche Kinderlieder

KLAVIERAUSZÜGE
VOCAL SCORES

Johann Sebastian Bach:
Johannes-Passion
Matthäus-Passion
Weihnachts-Oratorium
Magnificat

Georg Friedrich Händel:
Der Messias

Wolfgang Amadeus Mozart:
Requiem

KAMMERMUSIK
CHAMBER MUSIC

Cello Meets Piano I–II
Flute Meets Piano I–II
Violin Meets Piano I–II

© 1995 for this edition by Könemann Music Budapest Kft.
H-1093 Budapest, Közraktár utca 10.

K 115/4

Distributed worldwide by
Könemann Verlagsgesellschaft mbH, Bonner Str. 126.
D-50968 Köln

Responsible co-editor: István Máriássy
Production: Detlev Schaper
Cover design: Peter Feierabend
Technical editor: Dezső Varga

Engraved by Kottamester Bt., Budapest:
Balázs Bata, János Bihari, Éva Lipták, Zsuzsanna Geday

Printed by Kossuth Printing House Co., Budapest
Printed in Hungary

ISBN 963 8303 28 X